A Courageous, Clever Crow
Be Happy!

Art & words by Deborah Bradbury

A Courageous, Clever Crow - Be Happy!
Copyright © 2024 by Deborah Bradbury 🅱

Audience: Ages 3-7

ISBN: 978-1-0686108-9-9
www.deborahbradburybooks.com
@DBradburyBooks

All rights reserved.
No portion of this book may be reproduced or utilised in any form or by any means - electronic or mechanical, including photocopying or recording, or by any information storage and retrieval system - without written permission from the author

Acknowledgements
Once again, I want to express my heartfelt gratitude to my amazing husband for your continuous support. Your ideas and contributions are always invaluable to me.

I express deep appreciation to my four wonderful children, Carmen, Carolina, Danny, and Claudia, for consistently being my pillars of support and a source of constant encouragement.

This book belongs to:

All the precious children out there!

Can you find me in the book?

Deep in the forest beside a lake where the Courageous, Clever Crow lives, a group of animal friends prepare for an Easter Egg Hunt.

They decorate their nests with bright, colourful flowers and place pretty banners on the trees.

The little bunnies also take part and help out by carrying enormous eggs in big, wooden barrels to the Egg Hunt.

However, not all the eggs make it to the Egg Hunt as some bunnies like to hitch a ride!

The three little Crows, Coco, Casper and Cash, design beautiful Easter bunny hats to wear.

"Do you like my Easter hat?" asks Cash.
"I do love your bunny ears Casper!"

"Thanks, Cash. You look great too!" Casper replies.

"You all look fabulous!" remarks the Courageous, Clever Crow. "I love Easter. It's my favourite time of the year."

"Why is that?" Coco asks.

"Because for me spring is a happy time. It's like saying goodbye to the cold and hello to the warmth and new life!" replies Crow. "Plus, we get to do exciting Egg Hunts!"

"Well, I would much prefer to be one of the bunnies hiding the chocolate eggs. Then I would know where they were hidden! - I NEVER find any of them" Coco yells as she sadly wanders back to her nest.

"Oh, Coco. Be Happy! It's Easter."
Crow cries.

"Poor Coco! We must do something to make her feel better." Casper whispers.

"I have a clever idea! Why don't we secretly plan a surprise Easter Egg Hunt just for Coco?" Suggests Crow.

The following morning, Crow and his animal friends gather to start the Easter Egg Hunt.

As the hunt begins, they stand eagerly with their baskets waiting for the first clue to be announced!

As Coco reads her first clue, the Courageous, Clever Crow carefully keeps a bird's eye view!

Clue 1

Go to where the trees stand tall, your egg hides near something small.

Coco quickly finds her first clue. She reads it carefully then looks around for something small. Wait, be careful Coco! Something is lurking in the forest - be aware!

Coco is getting very clever at solving her clues and soon begins to fill her basket with Easter eggs!

Ah ha! Coco exclaims proudly as she spots the next clue.

She walks towards the cool, blue lake and wonders where this one will take!

Sailing across the Lake Merrily, Coco shouts with glee, unaware of the dangers that surround her!

Oops! An Easter egg drops and hits Peter Pike on the head!!!

Coco picks up her floating Easter egg and heads off to find her next clue.

Oh dear! The rock dropped by the Courageous, Clever Crow has knocked out Jiggly Jaws the snake!

Coco looks carefully but cannot spot an Easter egg! The clue proves challenging, yet she catches a glimpse of something pink. What could it be?

Coco is amazed that she has found all her chocolate eggs but soon discovers that her friends have none.

"Oh, look! I did it. I found all my chocolate eggs!" Coco screams with surprise.

"But where are your eggs?" Coco asks, confused.

You've found all the clues Coco. Well done and happy Easter!

Coco's friends congratulate her and praise her for successfully working out the clues on her own.

EASTER I SPY

HOW MANY?

www.deborahbradburybooks.com

EASTER EGG HUNT DESIGN

www.deborahbradburybooks.com

Deborah Bradbury

About The Author

Deborah Bradbury boasts over fifteen years of expertise as a primary teacher and is a proud mother to four beautiful children. She has a tireless passion for storytelling and a deep love for literature. There was never an evening without a bedtime story at home, nor an afternoon without a Roald Dahl book in class. Her love of children has inspired her to write stories that are engaging, educative, and fun for children and their families.

An advocate of reading, Deborah is passionate about cultivating a life-long love of reading in the very young. In class, she teaches her pupils that reading helps you become a creative writer, entices your imagination, and takes you on interesting journeys.

Deborah was born in Manchester, in the United Kingdom. She now resides in Spain with her husband, cats, and her dog, Spike. She speaks two languages and spends her free time cycling and playing squash.

If this Picture book left you enchanted, don't miss out on the next one in this series.

Collect the Courageous, Clever Crow Picture books now!

www.deborahbradburybooks.com

@DBradburyBooks

www.ingramcontent.com/pod-product-compliance
Lightning Source LLC
Chambersburg PA
CBHW041443010526
44119CB00042B/492